PREHISTORIES

Peter Scupham

PREHISTORIES

London
OXFORD UNIVERSITY PRESS
NEW YORK   TORONTO
1975

Oxford University Press, Ely House, London W.1

GLASGOW NEW YORK TORONTO MELBOURNE WELLINGTON
CAPE TOWN IBADAN NAIROBI DAR ES SALAAM LUSAKA ADDIS ABABA
DELHI BOMBAY CALCUTTA MADRAS KARACHI LAHORE DACCA
KUALA LUMPUR SINGAPORE HONG KONG TOKYO

ISBN 0 19 211846 3

© *Oxford University Press, 1975*

*Printed in Great Britain by
The Bowering Press Limited
Plymouth*

CONTENTS

ACKNOWLEDGEMENTS

Some of these poems have appeared in *Antaeus, Candelabrum, Caret, Encounter, Gong, Granta, New Statesman, Outposts, Poetry Nation, Poetry Review, Phoenix, Priapus, New Poems 1972–73* (P.E.N. Anthology, Hutchinson, 1973), and *The Best Poems of 1970 and 1972* of the Borestone Mountain Poetry Awards (California).

Ten poems were first published in a Keepsake Press collection, *The Gift* (1973), and two in Phoenix Pamphlet Poets No. 16, *The Small Containers* (1972).

West Country

THE Grand Bard's wreaths and rituals decay,
Those sky-blue robes, archaic lexicons.

His old house bleaches among shoals of hay,
Voyaging nowhere all the summer long,

Worked by a dynamo of sentenced bees
Lodged in a cave under our bedroom sill.

As yet, their tongue needs no revivalist;
The walls thrum to a doomed plainsong.

We grieve upon their notice of eviction
Whose hive will congregate no sweetness.

All tenancies, save one, are held on lease.
We claim our native element's forbearance,

Yet stony seas leach out a dying tanker,
Languages founder, Lyonnesse goes down,

And the Bard lies under slate in Zennor churchyard
Whose fingers carved unsinkable trim ships.

Old night, I know you at this quiet fabling,
Your crickets sprinkling their light vocables.

Life goes barefooot on this stubbled garden:
A hidden sea is talking in its sleep.

Beyond the lackwit stones, the granite faces,
A sisterhood of cows makes cavalcade.

Badgers possess this place; they come for alms,
Noble antique beggars in grey fringes.

I smile for you, you small ones at my feet,
Tying soft webs of trill from stem to stem.

We make no shadows in this august starlight;
We rhyme softly, each out on his limb.

Jimp saltatoria, brown grass-dancers,
Little, they say, is known about your histories.

Male and female he created them. Sweet love.
The girls have ears. Only the boys can sing.

Sun sets here in a damp quarter,
Yet one is conscious of bones:

Snapped sticks, angularities of guttering,
The shaft and tines of a worn fork.

The apple tree's articulation gathers
A sage and silver lichen;

Beneath her branches, one sunk boulder
Heaves a mossed and buffalo flank.

Furred husks of bees lie drily tumbled
Under an entangled window.

Bracken whispers, her corrugations
Brittle and simple as old fossil fish,

And the ribbed water tank is bare;
She sings and tremors windily.

The blood's course falters at the foot:
We wither at our slow extremities.

Public Footpath To

BEYOND the dented churns, the huddled farmyard,
Look, a green and lackadaisical finger
Reveals a hair-line fracture in the land.

Cold mud glints, beaten to a pale rivulet.
Button your coat against a change of season,
The sour attentions of a bramble frond.

Pause, lost, the thread absorbed by close-knit ploughland,
Stooping, unpick that crumpled fabric, palming
A broken tile, a freckled knob of bone.

Feel the chill rising : from damp skins of leaf-mould,
The swell of ground picked clean by flocking magpies,
The sodden beech wood clasping the dark hill.

Such slim capillaries, such seams and crinkles,
Overflown by clouds, nodded at by thistles,
Sealed by the impress of lost summer girls

And men whose ways were set by dawn and sunfall,
Offer a sense of flowers, endurances.
Time has stopped dead in their forbidden tracks

Where rank disordered trees and sniffling grasses
Huddle and fuss among the wind's rough twitchings,
Crumbling mouths yawn dimly at a hedge-foot.

Though a church tower makes her slight invitation,
Horizons alter as the bruised air thickens.
Let the past keep her right of way, while you

Are sensible, treading familiar ground again,
Of labouring barns, one self-sufficient tractor
Dragging the sullen landscape down to earth.

Ploughland

THEY drudged across the season's palimpsest,
The feathered horses, driven into rain;
Their dapples and attendant shades impressed
Upon the skies which pulled them up the lane.
    Light moves about the knotted ploughland, sown
    With undistinguished seeds of chalk and bone.

A sullen field, pegged out with brittle trees,
A water colour of the English School;
Her pawky hedgerows crumble to their knees,
The locked fires in her fractured flint lie cool.
    Old weathers broke her in, and we retrace
    The crows' feet etched on her dissolving face.

The lost teams and their leaders. All that care
Is mere commemoration by the wind.
A shower of bells freckles the cooling air;
Our booted feet drag with an awkward rind.
    Down in the levelled churchyard a few graves
    Remind the birds how well the past behaves,

Working along the bent flow of the land
With no more substance than our thought makes good:
A face limned on the air, a tenuous hand
To scribble in the margins of the wood.
    A rash of brickwork rubricates their claim:
    A foundered house, and a forgotten name.

The Home Farm lacked a tenant forty years,
Pigs littered grandly in the living room;
The rain is flighted with her children's tears,
A burnt tree's crater beckons to the tomb.
    One old man with his dog slows up the hill;
    A shooting party spaces out the chill

Where scatterings of green remind the day
Of beasts long cropped and felled: the molten dead
Still driving purpose through the common clay
In new returns of sacramental bread.
    The harnessed bells ride out upon their round,
    Tossing cold heads above the burdened ground.

Excavations

*'Time which antiquates Antiquities, and hath an art to make dust of all
things, hath yet spared these minor Monuments.'*
Sir Thomas Browne, *Hydriotaphia: Urn Burial*

1 Holwell

MONPAZIER relinquished a noble axe,
Lightly buried in an ochre pavement.

Holwell ruffled her ponds, lent an ammonite;
I tighten a mesolithic hand, follow a spiral,

Beat out the boundaries of withered oceans,
Quarry for silence under austere skies.

Land pulls down her unworked galleries,
Gathers her secret filaments.

There are gifts for the hacked acres;
Return is made, here where wind weeps ash,

The dump smoulders. Her stomach rises.
Fumes are exhaled from life's refusals.

A numinous machine in Monster Field
Chokes her gullet on a tip of spoil.

We annotate the scriptures of the hills,
And leaves close on half-burnt offerings.

2 *Taylor's Hill*

On home ground
We make frog garden:
Spades are trumps.

The skin strips
To a prickle of china,
Brick and slipware.

Earth recycles
Each old breakage.
Sixpence for the pudding.

Take her in the flank
With newsprint, sheeting,
Colonial fish.

Sun works hard.
Life breaks open
The surface tensions.

Under the lily pad
Old Leopard Spots
Crooks a long leg.

In autumn, drain her.
Frog's progeny peer
From high-rise flats.

3 *Welwyn*

A DUAL carriageway of chalk and mud
Betrays earth's tender hoardings.

Willow-herb, abundant on the site,
Seeds a vivid life on sufferance.

Yellow machines drone their defoliations:
Give me a lever, and I will move the world.

Exhausted aeons flare; life melts away
In a pother of bluish dust. The wind

Flutters a gay festoon of plastic pennons.
These towering inclines are defensible.

From half a bridge, a missed connection,
I consider this arterial surgery.

The land's bones lie in disarray;
Unreadable, her draughty palimpsest.

A new imperium holds, where scholars came
To grub for broken Rome with hasty fingers.

4 Harston

ROUGH chalk bowl,
The Sunday Army
Filled her full of lead.

She took it well,
Twisting their noses.
No more drill.

Just a bit older,
Scrub and sapling
Sweeten her neglect.

Her face dislimns,
Parting at the seams,
Molten in rain.

Leaf-moulds foster
New archaeologies:
Shell-case, punched can.

A silence of skulls
Where we once sat;
Felt air cleave

As wingtips kissed,
Pain touched down
From a canopy of sky.

5 *Sopwell*

A NUNNERY and mansion coinhere,
Enclose their orders in this tangled ground.
The site is intricate, and we must bare

Some Old Foundation nettle-rash implies.
The wild boys daily bring her to her knees,
Unlock the last bricks jigsawed to the sky.

The great reductions made, earth holds all close,
Shrinking her gums on Clio's wisdom teeth:
Height must be gauged from this impacted base.

We peel each layer through to yellow clay,
Build suppositions on that anchorage.
Hands ache with diagnosis. A hard case.

Slowly, the sun dries out the stones we skin;
Entrenchments deepen, and the shade extends.
We drink our tea and scour the shovels clean.

Salvation, if by works or faith, is toil.
A grace for the quiet dead, to work their bones
To pencilled lines: slight, yet more durable.

6 Cabinet

EACH virtuoso displays
A Cabinet of Curiosities.

Earth gilds unguentaria,
Gives bronze patina,

Expending ichor
To bring Baraka.

She holds long leases,
Profits by losses.

Loving cups and rings
Make funerals weddings.

Like Doctor Hans Sloane,
Earth refuses none;

Hunts down her fauna
With Collector's mania.

Let Walpole chaffer
Over Strawberry Fair,

Or graver Browne
Cogitate on an Urne;

She yields without demur
Keepsake and souvenir,

Asks no security,
Proud of her memory.

Her price suits all means:
A few gift-wrapped bones.

No cabinet, no virtuoso,
Can put it all on show.

7 *Font de Gaume*

THE ice has shifted, woods in equipoise
Weigh on the tumbled hillside. All's unchanged
Since the first savants of the limestone ways

Edged backward footsteps to where Font de Gaume
Lowers a cold hemline, inch by pleated inch,
And the slow zeros count the mileage gone.

The cavern breathes us in, and hushed we move
Towards our origin, a drift of children
About the two black nuns reserved by love.

We make obedience. The crisp words tell
Of shapes and limits scholarship has set
To counter sorcery with a shutting spell.

Fluent and grave, the ancient beasts release
Our loves and hatreds. High above our heads
The scarred rock sweats dull ochre, manganese;

Forms tremble and dissolve. We close to find
That heads are missing, horns become obscure.
Absolute zero : we begin and end.

8 Rouffignac

ROUFFIGNAC, Cave
Of a Hundred Mammoths.
C'est magnifique . . .

But it is the station!
A little blue train
Pulls you up and down.

We sit there solemn,
Off to see the pictures.
Electrics hiss.

Earth did it by herself:
No detonations,
Broken pick-helves.

Masonic water,
The Grand Quarrymaster,
Undercuts us all.

Candled graffiti
Sprawl huge cages.
Kilroy was here,

Killing off mammoths,
Seven at a blow
On the nursery frieze.

9 *Hauxton*

WILLOW and osier take possession now
In a field of stones, dug out for victory.

I take the vanished cat-walk over the pits,
Feel the heavy belting slope towards me.

Black cycles of time: an endless drudge
And hoist of labouring iron. Recurrences.

A coarse rush of pebbles and water
Churns and stirs in the grilled cylinder.

I hear again that antique grind,
The flails threshing a cold harvest.

Perched on a conglomerate of rust,
I finger a belemnite's unthreaded needle

And the chaff flies. Where are the screens
To wash and filter these memorials?

The gravel throws its cataracts away;
The room shakes to these dislocations.

CHOPPED planes lower
To a dark mouth, rimmed
By a calcite frost.

At Limeuil, limestone,
The perfect rock,
Has golden opinions.

The eye remarks
A lizard, armorial
On his baked ledge.

Heat flutters the air.
Blues and Browns
Drift on their nerves;

Settle on spurges.
Hawk moth larvae
Ripen into their skins,

Their Joseph coats.
I feel the fret
Of their neat mandibles.

Declensions of sun.
The unshut mouth
Aches in drought.

OUR fertile soils wander ever downward.
Substance makes removal; the waters take her.

The ground is suffering. Quake and crater
Wrench out, reaching for equilibrium.

She contorts her memories. Her strata
Suffer displacement and oblivion,

Vertical and horizontal fold,
Thrust fault and overthrust.

Innumerable, the bedded points of life
Preserved by a light sift of detritus.

Fresh resin swells the mould; out of decay
We pick the inscription on the heart of stone.

Marcasite breaks out her iron nodules;
Her silver secrets crumble and rust.

Older and deeper still, those massive rocks,
Granites, whose only life is central fire.

Life and Letters

A FATHER black-advised, takes the whip hand;
Hawthorn sways towards the scented dog-cart.

Chambers of maiden thought : annunciations.
A white sail, caught by wind and sun.

The noble folio is dragged guilty home
In fine exchange—a supper for a song.

Catullus breaks his old bones into flowers;
The staggering pagans bare each marbled nerve,

And one impossible She, with silly fingers,
Turns down his crisp and undefeated pages.

Released from Daedalus' restraining hand,
Icarus could spin the sun into the sea.

LONDON deploys her iron labyrinth;
A Minotaur bites Ariadne's thread.

The work drives counter; cut across the grain,
Coarsens to acclamation or neglect.

A siren chorus at the Mermaid Tavern
Proclaims who's in, who's out : court news.

The new wounds ache, though harshly cauterized.
His old friends break like promises.

Nature steals back her dumb replenishings,
Easing regretful lyrics, anodyne.

Unreasonable tears. Each midnight shows
The scales at their dark equipoise.

3

THE silences become remarkable;
His long walks dwindle to a turn.

Glad, now, to pause for music in the Abbey,
Caught faintly by the sloped woodlands.

Regret gathers for that long estrangement,
The one he could have shared all with,

Dead, exiled, or living unfrequented:
Some Chinese hermit with his scroll-work.

Time to arrange for the marmoreal fictions:
Truth some autumnal bonfire will consume.

A glacial and obsequious moonlight
Frosts out his hair, his favourite Cymbeline.

The Look

THERE was a quiet pressure in her face,
And when she raised her head, the stumbling look
Delayed upon the air : such alabaster
Closed up the crowded room like a dead book.
Her hair unwound its copper interlace.

A sketch of fingers working softly there
Unfolded a slow talk of cage and tower;
She overheard their private languages
And let each small, assuaging gesture flower.
She wore a silence that she would not share.

No matter now what the piano played.
Resolved antinomies of black and white
Lent a disguise of order to the hour.
The window spaces wept a morning light
Upon the trembling our assembly made.

He, ignorant of her white scrutiny,
Hoarded his brown and crumpled bones askance;
Hooded his mouth and eyes against the pulse
That beat inside the music or the glance,
Those looks that sent him wreaths for sympathy.

Then nothing which he had, and chose to give,
Weighed out an absence colder than a stone.
The grace-notes and the sunlight let them go.
Her fingers knew a way to live alone;
His dark, refusing eyes a way to live.

Birthday Triptych

BIRTH days: as of the spirit.
She cannot dissemble.
We break a fiery bread.

How should we navigate
The waves' coarse turmoil
Without appointed stars?

A luminary day, then.
Light of the first magnitude,
Confirm our chosen course.

Tides, in their slow recession,
Delay about your fingers
A light sweet freight of shells.

When fresh seas break,
May that beached miraculous wrack
Still hold its water lights.

On this your name day,
Under Janus, God of thresholds,
Past and future both become you.

2

THE true gift claims us.
Look! The flowered paper
Spills and crinkles.

A drift of white tissue:
Snow wreaths in May
We missed last winter.

And the small sign disclosed
Says in a new voice:
I tell of love in the world

To steady and delight you.
A long draught fills our horn;
We cannot exhaust her.

We read a common language
Runed in each offered hand.
Here, riddles are their answers.

Eyes rehearse tender cues.
All images compose and celebrate
The selves we have become.

3

NONE can walk safely.
The roads are dark, unsigned,
The sky precariously blue.

We must endure
Flowers, the rain's refreshment,
Each beautiful absurdity:

Accept with clear laughter
The dissonance of white hair,
Pain at the source.

A tree shakes at your window
Her brilliance of leafwork,
Admiration heals us.

Our vulnerability preserves.
To counter such a strength
Time's tactics have no skill.

Love sustains. By this avowal
We cancel fear, whatever tremors
Approach us from the bowed horizon.

Conclusions

WOULD you try conclusions with me, whose racing tongue
Makes terminus to your most speaking silence,
Scenting the air with absence, a sift of tomb-dust?

In these wild chemistries, I must become a child;
Rehearse again, as once in tattered schoolrooms,
Distinctions of suspension and solution.

I remember how your cut flowers, sapped of comeliness,
Stood in a stiff perch, their own conclusions drawn:
A suspension to subdue the vase that held them.

Now, your bright gift-look, lost between light and shade,
Dissolves in the summery air's mild crucible:
A solution to subdue my dark insistencies.

I would try conclusions with you, whose floated silences
Make terminus to my most faltering wordscape,
Scenting the air with presence, a sense of seed-time.

Demure

I AM most taken by this demure mood, lady:
The gentle voice with which you ease the air.

Calmly you gather to yourself, float lightly
On your ridiculous gay cushion's crochet-work,

Genie-borne through some dark Arab night,
Poised gravely in your own space and time.

The room darkens: lustre in your hair, your eyes.
Friends talk nothing in a language of ciphers,

Their words lent meaning by your meteor smiles,
Paradoxes of transparency and disguise.

I make small gestures to these formal ghosts,
My spirit bruised against your mysteries,

Caught, and held centreless at your point of balance:
A woman's wisdom, a child's innocence of repose.

May

She holds remembrances, anticipations.
A cold wind stood against me in the street.

Perverse to conjure up an alien weather,
As if each trembled blossom were pure crystal?

No, let us smile at such stage-management,
Crossings of blue and white with fitful grey.

The curtain rises to a gathering chorus:
A rush of ancient birdsong to the head.

Your month: a ministry of all the talents.
I watch you shake your laughter out together,

Going most gentle with your unfledged creatures,
A stumble of minikin cats, a quivering pond.

And in her green-room, you, the appointed May Queen,
Rehearse new cues for a long summer's play.

Landscapes

TWINNED landscapes travelling under the one sky,
Valleys and hills chequered to the one cloudscape.

Green and incurable, our child looks,
Which tell each other simple, yet true, fables.

When shadow draws you, your pensive face
Drifting among that dear abundant hair,

I too am caught by night's grave transience,
A native of your element of darkness.

And when clear light breaks, we rejoice together,
Delighted dancers in each other's laughter.

Let the glass fall, to daunt fair-weather friendship;
We dare four winds. Unlock your balm and snow.

Summer Ghosts

WE are the small ghosts of summer,
Eavesdroppers on the chit-chat of her clouds:

Our faces enigmatic as folded maps,
Our bodies a mere thickening of sunlight.

Butterfly hands, hovering, mating,
Smiles haunting the stiff green wheat.

Air smooths our voices into new textures;
Grass keeps no memento of our impress.

We procreate our deepest solitudes,
Scan the eyes' horizons for a sign.

Harvests intensify: a sense of gold.
How may two ghosts ripen into substance?

As If

As if the dying chapel in her grove,
With a most inward look, turned a blank face
To sunset and the lucencies of parting.
Then, briefly, let her golden surfaces
Enrich the air with generated light.

As if the clouds became the darkening sky,
And one wild bush, trembling upon the night,
Shifted the airs about and roundabout,
True author of the rain's diverse commotion.

As if such native sleight-of-hand is yours,
Performed, though, to an astonished daylight.
Some gifts confuse all reciprocity.

Wind and Absence

Down wind, down wind, a soft sweep of hours
Trawling in time. My pulse races into darkness.

Adrift, I draw your absence close about me;
Take the small ghosts of your hands to mine.

Your voice, your smile: such *son et lumière.*
My nerves conduct you round my floodlit bones.

Certain salt-water fools pester my eyes:
I stub them out with rough, dumb fingers.

The wind rehearses idle punishments,
Shaking a crush of unrecorded leaves.

A long-dead singer clears his ashen throat:
You creep his old cold music into life.

Poems bite on their pains. Dismayed, I know
The lines are scored in poker-work: black fire.

The haunted room trembles at your insistency.
Small, ghostly hands, allay the air's distress

As wind gathers, menacing our naked spaces
In dead languages of distance and rejection.

Quarries

Yes, I have my silent places too:
Serpentine quarries of linked words.

I cut each poem from a living rock,
Shaping it to your own dear likeness.

In that long no-time, I am alive with you,
Your presence palpable about my bones.

The sense of your small hands is terrible:
They work with me in secret, and I tremble.

You move about my splintered labyrinths,
Fingers trailing a kind white flower,

Haunting these lost and intricate dark blocks.
Pygmalion, I kiss you into life

And you hold out your longing arms to mine:
Your eyes blur to my own hot tears.

Can our tower fall, disperse to the four winds,
Whose one foundation stone is love?

Divers

WE knew infallibly: love marked the spot.
Oh, charted faces, time-worn and marine!

After a year tossed among waves of hair,
Brimmed eyes and flotsam glances,

In a free fall, we leave the surface play
And work of light; traverse the permeable deeps

That close about our origins. All births
Are dumbly recognized in these slow worlds

Where silence and the beautiful darknesses
Drift and brood above the spirit's dancing floor.

In echoing cadences of green slow-motion,
We celebrate the ancient mysteries:

Combers for lost gold in a lodge of sand,
Amazed discoverers of our buried selves.

Close

AT the close of a long summer, slow green fires
Consume the wandering fly and the poppy's membrane.
Life dwindles to a vigorous wreckage of bleached grass.

Heavy shadows beat the lawns to a duller gold,
And children's voices at the cool rim of twilight
Break the horizon, sturdy as trees and spires.

Let our eyes disentangle, hands drift apart, my dear,
Tired with the careful weight they have long carried.
Our senses tremble at the season's change

To wake again, astonished by a russet harvest
Or the first sifting of a hushed snowfall.
We grow in darkness, groping for new light.

No Cause

No cause, no cause. Adrift, he felt limbs tremble,
His tight skin burn, and the untidy room,
Stunned by such rough assault, crouch watchful back,
A frigid sun dappling the chequered floor.

Far worlds away, the children's careless voices
Tripped and fell. Only the clock drove on
Its balanced monotone. In that harsh pause
She stood as numb as ice, the tears in check.

And all was alien, lost: the cup she held,
The dumb cat shifting on the sill
And the green garden-light beyond the door.
How could there be for this no cause, no cause?

Vertigo

WEARY of foundering in Victorian silence,
Where pale occasional lamps disperse the gloom,
We find the strength to make a slight transition
And pace the balcony beyond the room.

Hands on the elegant railing, we admire
The melancholic trees, the broken fence;
Below, the tussocks in the formal garden
Mourn for their topiaried lost innocence.

Then you, ingenuous, with cat-felicity,
Swing yourself lightly on the rocking bar,
Back to the lawns, your hands crossed negligently,
Conscious that certainty can lean so far.

I grip the rail, inconsequently know
The centres of our gravity misplaced,
While hands and hearts, in fair-ground convolutions,
Perform their ritual in measured haste.

The grasses hiss, and the lean wind displaces
Curled leaves that swiftly turn a madder brown.
I, stay-at-home, gaze where your body presses
The unrecalcitrant dark flotsam down.

But your inevitable fall delaying,
You tire, step delicately down, and stare
With mock solemnity, sly comprehension,
Through that deep emptiness of cheated air.

Annotations

LOVE's the plain text of all our lives—in fine,
She suffers annotation. Codes and bows
Make decorative stains, and summer spells
Charm lustred inks and waters high, then dry.
    We hoard a tideline wrack of cards and shells;
    The drawer spills over, and the album swells.

There's a brief eloquence; if yours or mine,
A kiss can rubricate her Book of Hours
Before a wicked gloss creeps round the page.
We blame our hearts on strangers when we find
    Her gutter margins crowd with lust and rage,
    Peeping and steepling through dark foliage.

Yet innocence persists, though we decline
To conjugate her single verb, to give.
One day, considering flowers' pillow-talk,
I found, pressed to the heart of some gilt book,
    A stiff and brittle silk. I took the stalk,
    And found the spectre of a rose could walk.

Signed, Sealed, Delivered

1 Signed

THIS Indenture made
Between Myself and Time
Witnesseth that

A chain of paper
Binds me lightly
To the gathered shades:

An Army Surgeon,
Publican, Spinster,
Clerk in Holy Orders.

I breathe their skins,
My passage contoured
By their footsteps.

They are engrossed
In ancient deeds,
A semblance of movement,

Their bounds delineated,
Drawn in the margin
Of these presents.

A brass clock ticks
In consideration of the sum
Of their dry gestures.

2 Sealed

A RUSTLE of leaves.
Wax deploys
Her scarlet heraldries.

Poppy and balsam :
Weeds climb rampant
On a green silk ground.

In confirmation of tenure,
The evening snails
Etch in silverpoint.

Cats attest ownership
With a dawn sacrifice
Of entrails, feathers.

I move between
All ghosts and creatures
Who set here hands and seals,

Their parchment skins
Secured in the grave's
Diminutive tenement.

Love is the fee simple
Of these hereditaments,
Messuages, appurtenances.

3 *Delivered*

WHO will give me
Receipts for the duty
I cannot pay?

What heirs, executors,
Unborn assigns,
Will own this burden?

Beneficial owner
Of a chancy sunlight,
A chestnut's shade,

I mark a trilling of wings,
Visitations of bees
In the unsown border.

Delivery comes.
Genius loci,
Your shrine topples.

Unborn machines
Ruminate on a sour rubble,
Doors lie open

To winds rising
And a rain descending:
To a foliage of clouds.

Talismans

1 Christmas Lantern

Such flim-flam: a hutch of crumbling card
And the light's composure. Still talisman,

I think of nights your lucencies beguiled,
While the house rocked to the soft blundering guns.

I set my heart upon your heraldries
Where snow lies faultless to a cobalt sky,

Counting your shaken stars, adrift on paths
Diminishing among your vivid pines.

Frail monstrance, with an old anticipation
I set you here above my sleeping children:

The branched reindeer at the huddled bridge,
The simple house, offering her candled windows.

For their eyes now, your most immaculate landscape
And all the coloured rituals of love.

2 Village Minstrel

THERE, boxed hugger-mugger,
A few sad fictions,
Lost grammars, dying bibles.

And Clare, in scuffed half-roan :
Blue tributary stains
Wandering the marbled boards.

'To Dr Darling, M.D.,
With the author's best respects
And most grateful remembrances.'

December, eighteen twenty-seven.
The rented Helpston acres,
A freehold tenement of words.

I hold his winter gift,
A light between each darkness.
Who list presume to Parnasse Hill?

I search the engraved eyes.
Who could wish him less
Than his own inscription?

On my reliquary shelf,
His undefeated gold
Takes to this latter sunlight.

3 *Marbles*

THEY lurk in unfrequented corners,
A milky Venus, banded Jupiter,

Their planetary motions and disguise
Adept at eluding Time's removals.

This cold and crystalline survivor
Invites a slight clairvoyance :

Cracked asphalt, warm to the hand,
A blur of birdsong and white flowers,

A summer child, making and breaking
His solitary, erratic ring.

Taw and Alley skip and tinkle;
An old blood-brotherhood re-forms

Where all the lost and pretty dancers
Play the light music of the spheres.

Emblem and scene : indissoluble.
A twist of sunlight at the core.

Behind the Figures

1 Earth

LOAM is friable:
A crumpled darkness
Lit by flowers

Whose candid petals
Dress with white
The lawn's hem.

A mower draws out
Ribbons of light;
Throws a green waterfall.

Baize table land.
The iron rollers
Grind her down.

Worms cast out
Their whorled pyramids:
Dumb signatures.

The bed glistens
To slug trails,
Porcelain shells.

She tells a secret:
A ripening chrysalis
Tickles the palm,

45

Works her sharp tip.
An imago shut
In a twist of shade.

2 *Air*

JANUARY night
Unfolds the slow
Particulars of frost.

The witch fingers
Of webbed icicles
Catch her breath;

She lays bare
A dog shout,
A branching nerve.

Scratch fronded glass:
The summerhouse
Is thatched with light.

Engrossed by cold,
A child perches
On skimble bones.

A retinal scar's
Familiar hieroglyph
Slides over

A new fretwork,
A chalk sky
Seeded with birds.

To powdered asphalt
Some will come
For stone ground bread.

3 Fire

SALAMANDER days.
Rising sun
Burns off the dew.

Tight raspberries break
A sweet meat
From bobbled flesh;

Embryo life
Pales and curls
At the molten core.

Gold bruises out
Sharp loganberries
To finger stains.

Windows exchange
A summer heliograph
Of light messages.

A burning glass
On a hand's back:
The ellipse tightens,

Kindles a dance
Of smoke veils,
A pale flame.

A black hole
Through which a world
Slips, and falls.

4 *Water*

A STONE bird-bath :
Fluttering wings
Fuss brackish water.

The old butt swells
Her iron ribs'
Cool breeding ground

Into the scum
Unshipped oars
Crawl and founder,

The grass legs,
Translucent wings,
Faltering where

Striated larvae
Pause and hang;
Filaments tingle.

A shadow play
Of green and amber
Lowers and fades.

The light takes
These gauze deaths,
Silk entanglements.

Loose gnats drift
Where their children
Sink and rise.

The Secret

THE wagtail's semaphore in black and white,
A diadem spider, tense on corded dew,
Globular clusters of slow snails, clambering
At the wall's foot:
The daylight, filled with speaking likenesses.

Yet the dusk found him clenched, all lost for words;
The landing clock, hummocked by shadow, knew it.
Then a blue print frock, loose and talkative,
Spilled, interposed.
The conversation hung by a friendly thread.

She turned. 'Is anything the matter?' 'No.'
Only the fluttering secret a child must keep
Safe for the cold white acreage of sheets,
The moon's barred face:
Cows in the dusk, floating their clouded tongues.

Rain, sibilant on grass, came troubling on.
At night, while the old house cracked its joints
Or shivered its dusty timbers, the fledgeling secret
Broke out its wings.
When morning sun glanced in, his bird was flown.

Convulsion

DRAGGED brutally from sleep by a long, alien cry,
We tense, give startled glances. Something pleads
With bleak demands to be assuaged or beaten down.

She trembles, sweats. Her round and vagrant eyes
Lack sight. We must control this random violence;
Oppose with helpless words this gift of tongues.

So strange an absence loosens every part
Of our close world. In the unfriendly light,
Doll, cupboard, chair stare blankly back at us.

Ice, not love, eases. Hands recall gentler skills;
Our voices falter. Calmed by her dull sobbing
We sit, stiffly. At the night's cold margin

Our house resumes its usual tentative posture.
Someone we know is back. Something has left us.
We realize how great a strength went with him.

Outing for the Handicapped Children

THE held boat rocks to the staithe. Cautious, absorbed,
The children coax their limbs to their intent.
Her crutch blinks in the sun. Cheated by absent muscles,
He sinks with dazed acceptance to the grass.
About them, nervous in the gentle air,
Hands hover and fuss, glad to be ignored.

The day swells, unfolds. Laughter, scattered talk.
We hoist through dripping locks, part the dry sedges,
Plotting a fluent course by trees and swans
While summer, soft and potent, blurs through the awning,
Soaking the varnished wood. Torpid as grounded bees,
Their dangled fingers comb the river's skin.

They manage, patient, share with buns and fruit
A shaming kindness. Tamed, drowsy, separate,
We offer them our slow unnatural smiles;
Tremble with intimations of their pain.
The day we gave, or stole, edges away;
The cool depths pull their faces from the light.

Home Again

PROPELLED through time and space,
We make re-entry here;
Breathe a known atmosphere.

Nothing is out of place,
And yet we find it all
Alien, inscrutable.

It seems we must accept
The shape things draw on air
Merely by being there:

The faded walls, adept
At letting criss-cross books
Paper over the cracks,

The stolid easy chair
That sags like a stone sill
Or worn memorial.

Since with this world we share
An old complicity—
We brought it to be,

Why is the look so strange
On mine, or my child's face,
Caught in a looking glass?

What base yet out of range
Can send instructions now
How to make contact, how?

Prehistories

ADROWSE, my pen trailed on, and a voice spoke :
'Now, you must read us 'Belknap'.' My book was open.

I saw their faces; there were three of them,
Each with a certain brightness in her eyes.

I would read 'Belknap'. Then a gardener's shears
Snipped fatefully my running thread of discourse.

And in my indices, no poem upon which
I could confer this honorary title.

Foundering in dictionaries and gazetteers,
I came there : Belas Knap, a chambered tomb.

The lips are closed upon that withered barrow :
A dummy portal, a slant lintel hung

Beneath a scalp of ruinous grass, her walls
A packed mosaic of blurred syllables.

ENTERING is a deployment of small silences,
Frail collusions and participations.

A scrape of some sad traffic on the ear,
Bird song at her old insouciance,

I pull these down into an underworld
Of images alive in their dark shelter.

Such corridors are tacitly inscribed :
Do not abandon hope here, but desire.

When old men's voices stumble down the lane,
They too must be my dry accompaniment.

There is a shrinking in each new encounter,
A heaviness attendant on the work.

The vanished bone sings in her shallow alcove,
Making a sacred and astounding music.

Ghosts are a poet's working capital.
They hold their hands out from the further shore.

3

THE spirit leans her bleak peninsulas:
Our granite words loosen towards the sea,

Or hold, by some wild artifice, at Land's End.
The Merry Maidens dance their come ye all,

Keeping time to the piper's cold slow-motion,
Their arms linked against the lichenous Sabbath.

And a menhir, sharp-set, walled about
By a dirt-farm, a shuffle of lean cows,

Accepts, as of right, our casual veneration,
All fertile ceremonies of birth and death.

I see you standing, the new life quick in you,
Poised on Chun Quoit into the flying sky.

There, in that grave the wind has harrowed clean,
Our children crouch, clenched in a fist of stone.